Legal & Disclaimer

The information contained in this book is not designed to replace or take the place of any form of medication or professional medical advice. The information in this book has been provided for educational and entertainment purposes only.

The information contained in this book has been compiled from sources deemed reliable, and it is accurate to the best of the Author's knowledge. However, the Author cannot guarantee its accuracy and validity so cannot be held liable for any errors or omissions. Changes are periodically made to this book. You must consult your doctor or get professional medical advice before using any of the suggested remedies, techniques, or information in this book.

Upon using the information contained in this book, you agree to hold harmless the Author from and against any damages, costs and expenses, including any legal fees, potentially resulting from the

Contents

Introduction

OCD is short for Obsessive Compulsive Disorder, a type of mental disorder that gives severe anxiety and fear to the sufferer, brought about by obsessions and compulsions that come from uncontrolled and unreasonable thoughts, images, or ideas. It induces repetitive actions in an attempt to relieve the extreme panic and trepidation.

As you can see in the example above, a person with OCD cannot control these feelings and the corresponding behaviors needed to alleviate it. And because they always feel like they are compelled to perform these "necessary" behaviors, they waste a lot of time worrying about irrelevant things resulting in emotional, social, and sometimes financial troubles as well.

People with OCD are usually loners, out-of-place in a crowd, and may look like paranoid or insane. However, it was observed by experts that they typically have extraordinary intelligence.

According to medical research, OCD strikes both male and female correspondingly. It means that it is not gender-related, and so it does not matter whether you are a man or a woman when it comes to OCD.

What is surprising, though, is the fact that it affects around one to three percent of the population of the whole world, which is an astonishingly large number. According to a research done by the World Health Organization in the year 2000, the disorder is three times more prevalent in America, Europe, and Africa than in Asia and Australia, although there are still no official studies to conclude that it is ethnicity or location-related.

OCD vs Perfectionism

Having OCD is different from being a perfectionist. Although a common symptom of OCD is to do things right every time and all the time, an attribute that is highly similar with a perfectionist, this does not confirm that a person has it.

OCD symptoms that are usually associated with perfectionism include uneasiness about precision and accuracy or always wanting everything to be exact, fixation to always remember certain information or things, extreme "just in case" attitude or being overly prepared, and having a hard time letting go of possessions that does not have any use or meaning any longer.

You may always want your things to be organized in a certain way or your house to be as clean as possible all the time, and yet these may simply be a personality trait and not OCD.

In general, the obsessions and compulsions of an individual with OCD harmfully affects his quality of life and those who are close to him as well. It is not just some cute mannerism or peculiarity that a person possesses or humors upon. The problems are real for those who are suffering from it.

If you think you have OCD, you will need to be formally diagnosed by a mental health specialist to validate if you are really suffering from this disorder.

Fortunately, there are a lot of modern treatments and therapies right now that could successfully help people with OCD.

Chapter 1: Signs and Symptoms of OCD

The common signs and symptoms of OCD include a wide variety of obsessions and compulsions that are fairly noticeable to the casual observer. However, it is also likely that a sufferer would only show signs of obsessions or just signs of compulsions.

You can basically classify the signs and symptoms of OCD into these two groups, which are explained in detail below.

Diagnosis Still Needed

In spite of all these, it is not guaranteed that a person showing the aforementioned signs and symptoms associated with OCD indeed has the disorder. An official diagnosis is still needed to confirm if a person truly has OCD.

The reason for this is because some of these signs and symptoms are shared with other mental disorders as well, such as autism spectrum disorder (ASD), attention deficit hyperactivity disorder (ADHD), obsessive compulsive personality disorder (OCPD, which is more of a personality condition rather than an anxiety condition), and post-traumatic stress disorder (PTSD).

In fact, it is easy to misdiagnose a patient with OCD as having another condition, like bipolar disorder, social anxiety disorder, Asperger's syndrome, dermatillomania, and trichotillomania.

Another possible symptom of OCD is depression, which is brought about by the patient's perceived lack of self-control.

Compulsions

Meanwhile, compulsions in OCD are recurring actions that a sufferer is forced to do because of his obsessions. These repeated actions relieve the anxiety and distress brought about by the obsessions, albeit temporarily because they are actually a long-term hassle to the sufferer.

There are also specific areas of difficulties for compulsions, and they are as follows: cleaning, checking, organizing, and controlling thoughts and emotions.

OCD sufferers also tend to keep on doing the same things over and over even when not in their own homes. For example, when entering a public restroom, he may still check if the door is truly locked again and again before using it.

Because compulsions are just actions that are repeated over and over only for the reason of alleviating obsessions, it disturbs or interrupts a sufferer's use of his own time.

It also affects his social relationships as it makes him appear weird or creepy to family, friends, and acquaintances.

There are also regular compulsions that one may notice from someone who does not have OCD. Some examples of these compulsions that are not really symptoms of OCD are having a bedtime routine, following religious rituals and old traditions, practicing a skill (like taking a jump shot in basketball – you do it again and again), and working in an assembly line in a manufacturing factory.

Although these activities are repeated, they are not forced on someone but are only a preference or a standard procedure to finish something.

The most common signs of OCD compulsion are:

- Repeated washing of hands or usage of hand sanitizers because of the fear of acquiring germs

- Repeated checking of the door if it is locked or the stove if it is switched off

- Persistent organizing and cleaning when he thinks something is off or not right

- Incessant whispering of a word or phrase to take his mind away from inappropriate sexual and religious thoughts

Obsessions

Obsessions in OCD are recurrent, continuing, and unwelcome impulses that cause great anxiety and agony to the sufferer.

And the only way that a person with OCD can relieve this incessant torment is to perform compulsive rituals. These obsessions are detrimental because they get in the way of normal, everyday living, such as having a daily routine, performing hygienic habits, and interacting with others.

Typically, these obsessions have specific areas of difficulties, like terror of being contaminated by germs, distress in becoming aware that something is not symmetrical, unwanted ill thoughts of others, and inappropriate thoughts that are aggressive, sexual, or blasphemous in nature.

Most of the time, the person suffering from it is actually aware of the absurdity and ridiculousness of his obsessions, but it seems like he cannot do anything about it.

His awareness of it increases the anxiety even more. Sufferers usually feel embarrassed, terrified, and disgusted of themselves.

The problem with accurately diagnosing someone with OCD is that obsessions have become quite normal in this day and age.

A person may become so obsessed with trying to maintain a clean room, or waking up at a certain time of the day every day, or even passionately following an actor or celebrity, and yet live his or her life normally just like everyone else.

This is not considered as obsessive-compulsive disorder, but rather just a regular obsession.

However, the use of the term regular obsession could actually be irritating for an individual suffering from OCD as they may feel that it is diminishing or belittling the trouble that they are experiencing.

The most common signs of OCD are:

- Dreading to be touched or to shake hands with other people because of fear of germ contamination

- Persistent worrying that he left a door unlocked or a stove switched on

- Extreme fretfulness when things are not aligned or organized in the right way

- Inappropriate, impulsive, and uncontrollable sexual fantasies and thoughts of religious obscenities

Chapter 2: Causes of OCD

Even with the many hypotheses and studies on OCD, experts have not yet clearly identified the particular cause of this disorder.

There are many theories, though, and it was assumed that the causes of OCD can be induced by a mixture of hereditary, biological, environmental, cognitive, and behavioral aspects.

Biological

Speaking of genes, one gene that is regularly linked to OCD is hSERT or the human serotonin transporter gene. This gene is a neurotransmitter, which is responsible for producing serotonin transporters in the brain.

The function of the generated transporter is to absorb excess serotonin once a nerve cell shares it with an adjacent nerve. When the hSERT works too quickly, a person is said to experience some of the symptoms of OCD.

Another gene that is suspected to be causing OCD is SLC1A1, or the glutamate transporter gene. This gene is actually comparable to hSERT, but, as the name implies, it absorbs another neurotransmitter, which is glutamate, instead of serotonin.

Cognitive

OCD is also presumed to be caused by psychological aspects, including cognitive and behavioral factors. The cognitive assumption revolves around how a person misunderstands his intrusive thoughts as negative or harmful to himself.

It was mentioned in the previous chapter that OCD sufferers typically have intrusive or unwelcome thoughts that are either sexual or blasphemous in nature.

These thoughts make him react in such a way that would eliminate them, such as chanting or humming. But if the person continuously interprets these thoughts as true and they are harmful to himself, he will go on with the compulsions.

Some experts theorize that wrong religious or sexual beliefs during childhood may have triggered these kinds of thinking.

Hereditary

There are scientific researches that seem to suggest that OCD is hereditary. This means that it is assumed that the disorder can run in a family and be passed along from generation to generation.

Studies have shown that around 45 to 65 percent of children diagnosed with OCD were acquired because of genetics, although the results are inconclusive. This is because in examinations of identical twins, most cases where one of them developed OCD, the other one did not.

It is also further theorized that genetics may have played a larger role if a person is diagnosed as a child than when he is diagnosed as an adult. Again, this is only assumed because no particular gene can be established as the exact cause.

Behavioral

Another psychological aspect is behavioral. It is different from the cognitive assumption in the sense that compulsions are not triggered by unwelcome thoughts, but rather by fear of specific objects or circumstances.

An example of this is the fear of being contaminated by germs, which leads a person with OCD to wash his hands over and over again. OCD patients typically settle in avoiding the object of fear rather than dealing with it head on. This results in their usual compulsions.

Environmental

Some environmental aspects are also taken into account in looking for the cause of OCD. Researches have shown that chronic stress and parental upbringing may be some of the external causes of OCD. Around 53 to 73 percent of the cases are recognized to include environmental causes.

How a person was raised up by his parents is also presumed to increase the risk of developing or not developing OCD in the future. Furthermore, it is said that if a person is continuously subjected to stress, the symptoms of OCD could just worsen.

Other probable environmental causes of OCD are relationship problems, sexual abuse, unexpected and significant life changes, death of a loved one, and terminal illnesses.

Chapter 3: OCD Diagnosis

Formally diagnosing OCD is essential for a patient to be treated properly and effectively. However, only certified medical experts such as a psychiatrist, psychologist, or any accredited mental health practitioner is allowed to give an official diagnosis of it.

Tests and Procedures

In order to arrive at a definite conclusion, the mental health practitioner will perform the following tests on the patient:

- Physical test – this includes neurological tests to examine whether the nervous system is damaged or if it is properly working. As mentioned in the previous chapter, neurotransmitters such as serotonin and glutamate can be the culprit in the disorder.

- Lab test – this includes blood tests, drug and alcohol tests, and a thyroid exam. Blood, drug, and alcohol tests are done in order to find out if the condition is chemically induced or not, while the thyroid exam is to rule out any problems related to it.

- Psychological test – this includes a comprehensive interview with a psychologist, deeply touching the patient's feelings, behaviors, and thought patterns. The mental health practitioner may also interview close friends and family members with the consent of the patient.

Diagnosis Standards

From the American Psychiatric Association (APA) and the Diagnostic and Statistical Manual of Mental Disorders (DSM), the standards for a formal diagnosis of OCD include:

- The manifestation of either obsessions or compulsions, or both.

- Repeated and incessant intrusive thoughts and urges as described by the patient.

- These intrusive thoughts and urges induce fear, which causes significant anxiety, stress, and social and occupational deficiency to the patient.

- The symptoms are not the result of drug or alcohol abuse.

- The symptoms cannot be exactly described as that of another mental disorder.

Mental health experts put lots of careful examination and consideration to be able to diagnose OCD correctly.

Intensity Levels

There are three levels of intensity when it comes to OCD, and they are:

- Mild OCD – this means that the patient experiences uncontrolled obsessions and compulsion for only an hour or less in a day.

- Moderate OCD – this means that the patient experiences uncontrolled obsessions and compulsion for one to three hours in a day.

- Severe OCD – this means that the patient experiences uncontrolled obsessions and compulsion for more than three hours in a day.

These intensity levels are based on the amount of time a patient is socially and occupationally impaired by his symptoms.

Chapter 4: Common Therapy Methods for Obsessive Compulsive Personality Disorder

There are several different therapy methods for OCPD and each of these has both positive and negative aspects. Ultimately, it is up to the patient, their families, and their health care providers to decide which treatment, and the intensity of that treatment, will work best for the patient. It is important to remember that the selection of a treatment method should only be made after consulting with a qualified professional who can help the patient make the best well-informed decision.

1. Psychotherapy

Psychotherapy is a therapeutic treatment based on talk therapy. A psychologist or psychiatrist develops a relationship with the patient and attempts to guide the patient towards a healthier mental state. In the case of OCPD, this therapy is typically aimed at the short-term relief of symptoms than on the long-term alteration of the patient's personality. This is due to the difficulty in altering a person's nature, which is often beyond the skills of the clinician. It is also unlikely that the patient will be willing to, or able to, pay for such a long-term treatment. This is especially true in light of the fact that, due to their highly stubborn nature, it is exceedingly difficult to change the OCPD patient's nature.

Therapy focuses on having the patients learn how to properly identify and realize their emotions. Most people diagnosed with OCPD are more in-tune with their thoughts, rather than their emotions. They may become so focused on their thoughts that they are completely unaware of the emotions they are experiencing. They can frequently have problems recalling what their emotions were during an experience, while they may recall exactly what they were thinking. Altering this pattern can have a noticeable and significant improvement for those with OCPD.

2. Hospitalization

Hospitalization of those with OCPD is relatively rare and usually unnecessary. The nature of their disorder does not regularly impact the daily lives of OCPD patients and does not typically represent a threat to the patient, or to others. However, there are instances wherein the patient experiences some extreme life event or stressor which triggers their disorder to the extent that it causes a significant impact in their ability to complete daily tasks. In this case, hospitalization may be necessary. Likewise, instances wherein the patient becomes paralyzed by their disorder, such as being unable to leave their bed or to stop their compulsive behavior, may require hospitalization. Thankfully, these instances are uncommon. What is important to note about hospitalization is that it is not a functional long-term treatment option for OCPD. While it is a viable way to address immediate short-term and severe issues, a longer treatment method will be necessary for the patient's management.

3. Medications

Medication is not the treatment option most psychiatrists would prescribe for those with OCPD. Medications can carry with them serious side-effects and there is also the possibility of a patient becoming dependent on the drug. However, in instances wherein the patient's daily life is being severely affected by OCPD but not severe enough to warrant hospitalization, medication may be a viable option. Medications have recently been improved by the development of drugs, such as Prozac, which have showed some symptom relief for those with OCPD. This indicates that these drugs could provide some measure of relief for those suffering from OCPD. This method, however, will only relieve symptoms and not treat the underlying disorder. Therefore, medication may be a viable short-term option for treatment. However, it should be replaced, as soon as possible, with a method better suited for the long-term.

4. Cognitive Therapy

Cognitive therapy is a form of psychotherapy that was developed by an American psychiatrist named Aaron T. Beck. Cognitive therapy is focused on the psychiatrist and patient working collaboratively to recognize and alter unhealthy or illogical thought patterns. Cognitive therapy focuses on testing unsound thought processes to help the patient realize the error of their thinking, and to eventually alter the patient's thinking pattern in a natural way. In the treatment for OCPD, cognitive therapy is more focused on managing the reaction of patients to the thoughts they have and not in stopping the thoughts themselves. This is a more manageable task for both the therapist and the patient and can alleviate the symptoms the patient experiences due to their disorder. Cognitive therapy is a good long-term solution for OCPD patients that can have a positive and long-lasting effect on their behavior. The negative aspect to this therapy is the relatively long treatment time needed and the cost for such enduring treatment. Pursuing this therapy for extended periods may be impossible for those with a limited amount of resources or a less than generous health insurance plan.

5. Support Groups

Support groups are readily available for those with OCPD and their loved ones. These groups can be found in local communities or online, depending on the preference of the patient and their location. As a treatment option, support groups are a mid-level option. Some patients may not be affected much by their OCPD. Thus, joining the support group might be the only treatment needed. However, patients who are more significantly affected by their disorder may need additional therapy in conjunction with the support group sessions. Nevertheless, joining a support group is highly recommended. Patients can find a valuable source of support there as well as be introduced to positive treatments or providers. They can also learn more about their disorder and gain an understanding of their condition from someone other than their health care provider. A simple web search will turn up many groups that patients may join, including **www.ocpd.freeforums.org** and **www.obsessive-compulsive-personality-disorder.meetup.com**. Both are free forums for those who suffer from OCPD and have a loved one who has OCPD.

6. Relaxation Techniques

The patient with OCPD is someone who is bombarded with stressors. They experience high levels of tension and anxiety which contribute to the aggravation of their disorder. Relieving some of this tension and anxiety can help the patient re-assert some measure of self-control over themselves and their disorder. It may also provide the patient with a chance to judge their compulsion from a more rational viewpoint, and possibly even rejecting that compulsion. In order for this to be possible, the patient may use relaxation techniques to help alleviate the tension they feel.

Relaxation techniques may include specific breathing techniques or even yoga poses, which fosters a sense of serenity in the patient and allows them to think past the immediate moment. The negative aspect to this treatment method is that the underlying disorder is, likewise, not treated. This means that while the patient may gain some measure of control over their compulsions if consistently applied, relaxation techniques will never end the compulsions themselves. The positive aspect of this treatment method, aside from the immediate relief provided, is that there is little to no real cost accrued when utilizing these techniques. There are multiple sources from which to learn the best techniques for a specific individual, such as those found online or at the local library. Another major benefit is that this treatment option can be utilized in real time. Whenever the patient begins to experience stress from their compulsive thoughts, he or she can make him or herself calm down and manage the symptoms. This is very much unlike other therapies which require a therapist, a pill, or some other secondary device for it to work.

7. Aromatherapy

Aromatherapy may seem like an odd treatment choice for OCPD. However, much like relaxation techniques, aromatherapy can help to relieve tension and stress induced by the patient's OCPD. Aromatherapy can be administered in a variety of ways, such as through massage with essential oils, and aromatic baths or vaporization. Certain oils and scents are used to provide relief for certain symptoms. Lavender, sandalwood, and nutmeg, for example, are all used to help alleviate stress. Vanilla, orange blossom, chamomile, and other floral scents are used to help relieve anxiety. Certain aromas may be better for some individuals than for others and each patient should find a combination that works best for them. The benefits of aromatherapy are very helpful in the relief of the symptoms experienced by a person with OCPD. However, like many other treatment options, aromatherapy is not a cure for the patient's OCPD and may need to be used in conjunction with other treatments.

Chapter 5: How to Choose the Right Therapy

OCPD may vary in intensity, from being a mild personality quirk that the patient and others learn to live with, to being a true challenge to the patient. OCPD is unique in nature in such a way that while these individuals experience difficulty as a result of their disorder, many of them lead relatively normal lives unabated. Individuals with OCPD can have successful careers, marry, have children, and enjoy friendships.

This variation is an important element in determining the right therapy. If the patient has a lower level version of OCPD, lighter treatment options may be better than high-handed tactics, such as medication or psychotherapy. Likewise, a patient with a severe case of OCPD that affects their day to day lifestyle is unlikely to gain lasting benefits from just joining a support group. More intense treatment methods may be needed in order for these patients, such as cognitive therapy. The first step in selecting the correct therapy for the patient, therefore, is to determine the intensity of therapy needed. Determining which level of treatment is best for the patient will require the help of a licensed professional who can bring an informed opinion as well as an unbiased view to the selection process.

After determining the intensity of treatment necessary with the help of a licensed professional, patients should research on their treatment options. Having an in-depth understanding of what a treatment requires, and what benefits and costs come with it, is an essential part of choosing the right therapy. A lack of knowledge can lead to serious mistakes in choosing the best therapy. For instance, a person who is unaware of the limitations of medication in treating OCPD may believe a prescription will 'cure' them. Finding out differently later in the treatment process can cause undue stress that may trigger greater symptoms from their disorder. While a professional health care provider such as a psychiatrist or psychologist can make recommendations regarding treatment, the patient is ultimately the only one capable of making that decision. Therefore, patients should be well-informed as possible on all treatment options before selecting the treatment path they wish to take.

In addition to determining the level of intensity the patient will require in their therapy and researching the treatment options available to them, patients should be aware of their individual preferences and realities. For example, if a patient is unwilling or unsuitable to learn and implement breathing techniques, the patient should focus on options that appeal to them more. There is little use in spending time and money on a treatment option that the patient feels uncomfortable with as they are unlikely to utilize it over the long term. On the other hand, focusing on those therapies which appeal to the patient the most will encourage the actual use of that therapy. Those who are interested in natural treatment methods may do better with aromatherapy, for instance, rather than with medications and vice versa.

This is not to say that choosing one therapy excludes another. Due to the type of therapies available to help treat OCPD, many treatment options can be used in combination with others to provide the best results. Those who opt for cognitive or psychotherapy treatments may also benefit from breathing techniques and aromatherapies. Regardless of the other chosen treatment methods, patients would also do well to join a support group. Joining such a group can have a very positive influence on the patient's outlook on their disorder while having a sense of belongingness and community. These and other combinations of treatment options should be discussed with the patient's health care provider. They may even create a treatment program guide that includes each of the options selected, including when and how to use them. This will provide the patient with a semblance of control that the OCPD patient needs to feel comfortable, while also providing valuable knowledge in an easy to access format.

This combination is not only for those treatment options which are less medical in nature. Psychotherapy or cognitive therapy may both use medications, if necessary, to help the patient overcomes difficult periods in their treatment. Hospitalization can also be utilized, if absolutely necessary, in conjunction with the other therapy methods.

Once the patient has selected the treatment option he or she would like to utilize, he or she should begin to research on potential providers for those treatments. While the patient is likely to have at least one mental health provider, the patient may want one or more additional providers to obtain access to less traditional forms of therapy. If this is the case, patients should first ask for a recommendation from their current mental health care provider. Most psychologists or psychiatrists will have a readily available list of providers with whom they associate with that may be able to provide different treatment options.

Even if the patient's current provider has such a list, patients should research on each name given to them before selecting. Checking each doctor's credentials, degrees, and reviews is a great step to take. Patients should also check the experience of each provider in working with OCPD patients. This should eliminate some of the providers the patient is considering. Scheduling an office visit with different care providers allows the patient to gauge the different styles and personalities of those whom they may be receiving treatment from. Patients should eliminate from the list those whom they feel uncomfortable with, or those who have a different treatment plan from what the patient has in mind.

The most important aspect of selecting a therapy, or therapies, is creating a combination of factors that allows the patient to live a normal life as possible. Selecting that combination should always be done with the consideration of the patient's lifestyle, personality type (aside from their disorder), preferences, and resources. Patients should feel comfortable with their health care providers and be at ease with the therapies they choose. As long as those requirements are met, the patients will be able to select the best therapy and the best provider for their needs.

Chapter 6: How to Overcome Obsessive Compulsive Personality Disorder

Overcoming OCPD may seem a daunting task for both the patient and for their loved ones. OCPD is a disorder that, in many ways, becomes the defining characteristic of the patient. OCPD patients may not know who they would be without this aspect of their personality, and frankly, many may be afraid to find out. However, for those who can see the problems OCPD creates for them, and for those who are brave enough to address them, OCPD is a manageable task. The keyword here is manageable. Overcoming a disorder as all-encompassing as OCPD is neither an easy task, nor is it a fast thing to do. Patients should be prepared for long-term treatment and lifestyle changes.

In order to overcome OCPD, patients must take several important steps. Recognizing that they have a problem to begin with is the first and, perhaps, most difficult step for OCPD patients. Most OCPD patients do not see a problem with their current lifestyle and they are reluctant to dramatically alter a fundamental part of their life. The reality is that OCPD does affect the life of a patient in a negative way. Many people with OCPD are missing out on essential parts of their life. They often fail to enjoy what little time they spend with their family. Furthermore, they may strain personal relationships or even damage their careers as a result of their OCPD.

The OCPD patient, however, often overlooks these negative aspects of their current lifestyle. When they do see these less than perfect situations arise, they may blame others or circumstances rather than see any problem with themselves. Patients should ask themselves the following questions to recognize that they have a disorder:

1. Do they allow their need for order and perfection to derail projects?

2. Do they become so engrossed in staying on schedule that they forget to enjoy their activities?

3. Does working through holidays, even when they do not have to, a common occurrence?

4. Are they reluctant to allow others to complete tasks for fear that it would not be done 'correctly'?

5. Can they remember the last time they truly appreciated how something made them feel?

Once the patient begins to accept that they have a problem, their next step is to seek out a professional mental health care provider. This professional, who should either be a licensed psychologist or licensed psychiatrist, will be able to formally diagnose the patient. It is important to remember that diagnosing or treating a disorder without the aid of a professional is dangerous and potentially costly. A person who fails to seek the aid of a mental health professional and yet proceeds to treat their disorder will most likely do harm to their self or spend thousands without seeing results. Enlisting the aid of a qualified mental health professional can prevent both outcomes.

The professional will be able to help the patient in more ways than just providing a correct diagnosis. They may be able to offer their own services and a treatment method depending on their skill set and experience level. Even if the patient's original provider is not capable of providing the needed treatment itself, they are likely to recommend others who will be able to do so. These providers will also be able to give the patient much needed information about their disorder as well as how to join a support group. Likewise, they will be able to present what treatment options are available for the patient and what each of these options entail. The most critical aspect of this step is ensuring that the patient chooses the right provider for them. Researching before selecting the provider is a smart idea. Patients should check for education levels, awards and certifications, patient reviews, and experience levels with OCPD before choosing their provider.

After enlisting the aid of a professional, OCPD patients should enlist the aid of family and friends. A personality disorder is something that does not only affect the patient but everyone around the patient as well. Likewise, treating a personality disorder takes more than just the effort of the patient but the effort of all those involved in the patient's life. Family members and friends can be valuable resources in battling OCPD. As the people closest to the patient, they are even more likely to recognize areas wherein the patient's disorder affects them more than the patient themselves. Speaking to those closest to them can help the OCPD patient understand what areas of their life they truly need to focus their treatment on. Likewise, it shall give the patient a sense of community and support in their effort to change themselves.

Moreover, these individuals can act as real-time alerts to the patient's disorder, giving the patient a perspective on their actions at the moment. This allows the patient to choose their behavior in a meaningful way. For instance, if a child informs their OCPD parent on a family outing that the parent is becoming overly caught in keeping things on schedule and not focusing on enjoying the family, the patient may be able to make a conscious choice to alter their behavior. This also allows those around the patient to gain an understanding of their behavior, potentially reducing the frustration they feel as a result of the patient's OCPD and hopefully improving the relationship.

Once the patient has spoken to his or her family, they should begin the treatment or treatments of their choice. The important element to this step in OCPD is realizing that the patient cannot overcome their disorder by themselves. Those with OCPD have a marked tendency to be both stubborn and loners by nature. This combination may lead the OCPD patients to draw the false conclusion that they can address their disorder without taking any of the treatment options available to them. This could not be more wrong. OCPD is not something that a patient can overcome by themselves. These patients will most likely not recognize when and how their disorder affects them. Treating their disorder effectively is way beyond the capability of most patients. Therefore, external help is absolutely necessary for the OCPD patients to overcome their disorder.

Not every patient needs the same type of treatment. Patients should utilize the opinion of their professional provider, closest family and friends, and their own good judgment to select the treatment option best for them. In addition to any treatment option the patient chooses, it would be a wise decision for both the patient and their family to join a support group. Joining a support group offers many great benefits to the patient and their family, including priceless information, a steady source of support, and a judgment free avenue to voice out frustrations that arise due to either the OCPD or the treatment thereof. There is little to no downside in joining these groups as they are generally free of cost and can be accessed either in person or online. Utilizing such a useful tool in addition to other treatment options may greatly contribute to a patient's success in managing their OCPD.

Overall, overcoming OCPD revolves around many different, yet equally important, elements, such as the patient's recognition of their disorder and their willingness to address this disorder, the help of a reliable and experienced professional in both diagnosing and treating the patient's disorder, the support of the patient's family and friends who will act as safeguards against old habits while supporting positive changes, and the utilization of the best treatment options available to the patient, including as many different avenues of treatment as necessary.

These elements work together to give the OCPD patient a formidable toolbox with four essential tools in managing their disorder. The patient's recognition of their disorder gives them awareness that they become cognizant of the underlying causes for their behavior. By seeking professional help, patients gain knowledge that they can utilize to make smart decisions in managing their disorder. Relying on friends and family provides the patient with a foundation of support to help them make the necessary decisions and changes in their lives needed to address their OCPD. Seeking treatment is a concrete action that will provide the patient with concrete results in managing their OCPD. These four tools (awareness, knowledge, support, and action) are all that the patient needs to successfully manage their disorder.

However, it is unlikely that a patient will be completely 'cured' of their OCPD even with intensive treatment. Patients will likely always experience compulsions due to their OCPD. What these OCPD patients should remember is that the ultimate goal in addressing their disorder is not to be 'fixed', but to enable them to live a normal life as possible. With the help of these critical elements, these patients should be able to effectively manage their OCPD impulses and live a more normal life.

Chapter 7: Relationships and OCD

More often than not, when a member of a family is diagnosed with OCD, other members would surely ask how they could be able to help. There are several efficient steps that families and friends can help a person with OCD.

First, families and friends need to educate themselves about OCD. They can do this by reading books on OCD; attending support groups dedicated to OCD; joining OCD foundations; and researching online among others. Families and friends should be able to realize that the more they learn about OCD, the more they can help their loved ones with the disorder.

Second, it is necessary for families and friends to acknowledge and reduce behaviors of family accommodation. These behaviors are associated with things that families do, which trigger symptoms of OCD. While it is true that OCD demands affect families, friends, and other relationships constantly, it is how they respond that possible sparks off OCD symptoms. Once families and friends learn the proper responses and impact of their behaviors to a loved one inflicted with OCD, they would be empowered to create stability among them.

Third, families and friends can help a loved one with OCD find the right treatment for the disorder. Although medicines and cognitive behavior therapy are considered the most efficient treatments, family support and education are likewise significant keys to treat OCD.

Fourth, families and friends can learn how they can respond appropriately to a loved one with OCD who refuses treatment. This can be done by offering encouragement to the individual. Say, families and friends can tell the individual that proper treatment causes a significant decrease in OCD symptoms. In addition, they can also tell the individual that there are others who are experiencing the same endeavor as theirs and that there is help. Offering encouragement may also include suggesting to the individual to attend support groups, speak to a professional in OCD, or talk to another OCD patient through online OCD foundations or support groups.

Families and friends can respond appropriately to an OCD patient by attending support groups where they can learn how to deal with the symptoms. **They can also obtain feedbacks and other pertinent information from other families who also have an OCD patient.**

Another way of responding appropriately to an OCD patient is **bringing materials with OCD**

information and leave it where the patient can read or listen on his/her own. These materials may include video tapes, books, and audio tapes among others.

Finally, one of the most efficient ways to respond appropriately to a loved one with OCD is to **obtain support and help.** It is best for families and friends to seek the support or advice of a professional in OCD cases. Speaking with other families who are undergoing the same problem can also help family members and friends to release whatever they feel about the OCD patient.

Problematic behaviors, relationships, and OCD

There are several problematic behaviors among families, friends, and other relationships that can affect a loved one with OCD. These include making changes in family routine; participating in a certain behavior; taking extra responsibilities; assisting in avoiding; making changes on a job; helping in a certain behavior; and making changes in leisure activities.

When it comes to making changes in family routine, this means that you can affect the behavior of a loved one with OCD by changing, say, the frequency of changing your clothes or changing the time that you shower in a day.

Participating in a certain behavior means that you go along with the OCD behavior of a loved one instead of correcting it. For instance, when the person suffering from OCD washes his/her hand, join in and wash your hands as well.

Assisting in avoiding means that you tend to help your loved one with OCD avoid things that distract, disappoint, stress, or upset them. For example, it is possible to try to wash their clothes for them thinking that you would be able to do it the right or proper way.

Making changes on your job means that you try to reduce your work hours so that you would be able to take care of your loved one with OCD.

Helping manage the OCD behavior of your loved one means you "tolerate" the behavior. For instance, if your loved one is fond of buying cleaning products, you buy for them in large amounts.

Finally, making changes in leisure activities means that it is all right for you not to leave the house unless you are with your loved one with OCD. Thus, apart from tolerating the behavior, you also let the behavior affect your time with friends, interests in movies, or dining out.

Chapter 8: Tools for Managing OCD at Home

In order to manage OCD effectively, it is best to start building tools that include strategies, which can help you in dealing with your obsessions.

However, you need to know the vicious cycle of OCD in order to come up with the right strategies. The OCD cycle begins with the trigger, followed by the obsession, and then you come up with the meaning of your obsession, and ends in anxiety.

On the other hand, you can start breaking this cycle by learning to eliminate or discard unhelpful coping strategies gradually. Unhelpful coping strategies include compulsions. Next, you should learn to balance your obsessions.

There are several tools that you can use in order to break the vicious cycle of OCD.

Tool 1: Face your Fears

One of the most efficient ways to break the cycle of OCD is to face your fears gradually. The technique that is used for facing fears is referred to as exposure and response prevention (ERP).

ERP is carried out through exposure to situations that bring on your triggers or obsessions. It is also done by not getting involved in unhelpful coping strategies such as avoidance and compulsions.

First, in order to face your fear through ERP, you should learn more about your OCD. You should be able to determine your obsessions and identify the triggers that result to your compulsions and obsessions. This can be done by keeping track of your triggers daily for at least a week.

Given that your obsessions can transpire frequently, you can write down 3 triggers a day, which will provide you an overview of your obsessions and compulsions. You can put labels to columns so you could rate the intensity of your trigger in a given situation. For instance, a column can be labeled as "fear" and rate its intensity ranging from 0 for no fear and 10 for extreme fear. You can then record your compulsions or other coping strategies to address an obsession. Make sure that you include both mental and/or behavioral strategies that you use in order to manage your obsession.

Second, you can make use of ERP to face your fears by building a "fear ladder." Once you have reached a week of tracking your obsessions and compulsions, you can make a list of all situations that you fear. You can then build a fear ladder by ranking your triggers based on their intensity, say, from least to most scary.

Take for example the fear of contamination. If you have fears of contamination, it is possible that the intensity is only 1 out of 10 when you are in a friend's house as compared to using the public restroom in a shopping mall. You may find that using a public restroom translates to a very high intensity of 9 out 10 on your fear ladder.

When building your fear ladder, it is best to separate a ladder for every obsessive fear you have. For instance, you may need a ladder for all related situations to your fear of contamination and another ladder for your fear of causing a terrible event to transpire.

Facing Fears through Exposure

As you face your fears through exposure, start with the easiest item on your fear ladder and increase the difficulty as you go along. Make sure to track your progress, specifically your level of anxiety, throughout the exposure drill. This would allow you to determine the decline of your fear on a specific situation.

When doing the exposure drill, make sure not to avoid your fears. For instance, do not allow yourself to make subtle avoidance by touching the doorknob with just one finger instead of using your entire hand; talking to someone; or thinking about other things. When you engage in avoidance, it would be more difficult to face and get over your fears.

Take your time as you try to expose yourself to your fears. Make sure not to rush when you are in a specific situation until such time that your fear declines by at least a half. In addition, focus on facing and overcoming the first item on your fear ladder prior to moving on to another. Do the exposure repeatedly for the first item until it no longer becomes a problem or hindrance for you.

Doing the Response Prevention

Exposure would only work if you try to resist engaging into your compulsions. This means you have to resist your urge during or after the exposure. It is important to take note that the objective of ERP is to be able to face your fears without carrying out your compulsions.

Meanwhile, it can be hard for you to determine a way to face a specific situation if you have been giving in to your compulsions for quite some time. As such, it is best to ask the help of a family member or someone close to you without OCD. Ask them to model their behavior, say, leaving home without having to recheck appliances over and over or washing their hands as quickly as possible. This way, you may be able to adapt how they behavior.

If you are facing your fears for the first time, it can be difficult to resist a compulsion completely, but you can delay and reduce your rituals. Instead of not doing the compulsion entirely, you can at least delay acting upon it. For instance, if you entered a public restroom (exposure), wait for at least 10 minutes before leaving. If you touched something that you think is contaminated, wait for at least 5 minutes before you wash your hands and do it for a minute rather than 3 minutes. It would be very helpful if you try your best to prolong the delay until such time that you are able to resist your compulsion totally.

In the event that you find yourself carrying out a compulsion, it would be best to re-expose yourself immediately to that same situation that you fear. If you have to repeat re-exposing yourself, do so until such time that your fear drops altogether. Say, if you entered a public restroom, stay there for at least 5 minutes. Leave and re-enter the restroom and stay for another 5 minutes before leaving. Do this repeatedly until your fear drops by a half.

If you experience only a little anxiety as you complete a drill, it is time to move on to the next item on your fear ladder. For instance, if you feel just a little anxiety when entering a public restroom and staying there for 5 minutes or more; challenge yourself constantly. Stay inside the restroom for as long as you can handle and leave. Do this challenge repeatedly until your anxiety goes away entirely.

Tool 2: Challenge and Replace Unhelpful interpretations of Obsessions

This tool can be very efficient when combined with Exposure and Response Prevention (ERP) in order to address your disturbing thoughts, which are all part of OCD.

Even for people without OCD, it is normal to have unpleasant or unwanted thoughts once in a while. Some may be very much affected or bothered by such thoughts while others may not. When you are bothered by an unpleasant or unwanted thought, it is because of the interpretation or meaning that you associate with it. Individuals with OCD have the tendency to perceive unpleasant or unwanted thoughts as important, dangerous, and meaningful while those without OCD may simply discard or bash the thought.

Take for example thinking that you might contract a serious disease because you touched something inside a public bathroom. For people who do not have OCD, they may simply find it weird for having such thought. Thus, they would not feel anxious and go on with their day.

However, if you have OCD, you automatically assume that it is highly possible for you to contract a serious disease when entering a public bathroom and touching something in it. You may even think that you can pass on the disease to your loved ones. Thus, this can make you very anxious, which leads you to giving in to a compulsion and starting the vicious cycle of OCD.

Consequently, it is vital to challenge unhelpful interpretations of your obsessions and replace them with helpful ones in order to manage OCD. As mentioned earlier, this tool can be very effective when combined with ERP.

How to Challenge Unhelpful Interpretations of Obsessions

There are 2 steps in order to challenge unhelpful interpretations of obsessions. These include knowing what you are thinking and managing your obsessions.

First Step: The first step involves knowing the interpretations you give to your obsessions prior to challenging them. You can start by tracking your obsessions and the interpretations or meanings you give to them. It is best to track them every day for at least a week. Keep track of at least three obsessions daily to provide you with a good overview of your pattern of thinking.

Record the situation that triggers your obsession under the "situation" column; obsessive thoughts in a specific situation under the "obsession" column; and all emotions you had as the obsession transpired under the "feelings" column. Make sure to rate the intensity of your feelings ranging from 0, which translates no emotion to 10, which translates to most intense emotion. Record your interpretations or meanings to your obsessions under the "interpretation" column.

You can determine the interpretations or meanings of your obsessions by asking yourself four basic questions. First, what the cause might be for you to be upset about a specific obsession. Second, what such obsession says about your personality or yourself. Third, what might be the kind of person you are if you did not have such obsession. Finally, ask yourself what might happen if you did not do anything about your obsession.

Second Step: The second step involves managing your obsessions once you are able to determine them as well as the manner of interpreting them. There are several sub-steps that you can do in order to manage your obsessions.

Sub-step 1: Learning the facts

It is normal to have unwanted or unpleasant thoughts although they can be annoying. However, these thoughts are harmless. Even if you have a specific thought, it does not mean it makes you a bad person or that it would come true. It is best to learn the facts about your thoughts and keep in mind that they are harmless unless acted upon.

Sub-step 2: Realistic Thinking

More often than not, adults with OCD have the tendency to fall into thinking traps just like others with another type of anxiety order. These thinking traps are often negative and unhelpful when it comes to looking at things. Thus, it is important to learn how to think realistically. This means that you have to look at all aspects of a specific situation including its positive, negative, and neutral aspects prior to making any conclusion. It is like looking at yourself and the world in a fair and balanced way.

Sub-step 3: Challenging Unhelpful Interpretations Of Obsessions Through General Strategies

In order for you to end up with a balanced way of perceiving your obsessions, ask yourself several pertinent questions:

Question 1: What are the pros and cons of your type of thinking?

Question 2: Are your interpretations about a certain situation realistic or accurate?

Question 3: What evidence is for and against a specific interpretation?

Question 4: Have you mistaken a thought for a fact?

Question 5: Are you 100% certain that your thought will transpire?

Question 6: Is your judgment based on your feelings instead of reality or facts?

Question 7: Are you confusing certainty with possibility?

Question 8: Is there a more rational way of perceiving such situation?

Once you are able to challenge your initial interpretation, you would be able to provide a balanced meaning to your obsession and replace them with calming and realistic ones. You would also find that challenging your interpretations can make you feel better. Although it may be difficult at first, you should not be discouraged. It is normal and expected to find it hard to believe the helpful interpretations you end up with at first; however, with constant practice, it will get much easier. You will soon find that your new interpretations are stronger than what you previously had.

There are several specific strategies that you can do in order to challenge some of the most common misinterpretations of obsessions. These include calculating the chances of danger, creating a responsibility pie, carrying out the continuum technique, and doing the survey method.

The method of calculating the chances of danger can help you be more realistic about the probability of your worst fear to happen. You should keep in mind that having a thought that something might happen does not mean it is true. It is important that you take note of your thoughts and determine if your OCD thoughts are unhelpful or wrong.

The responsibility pie can help you challenge excessive sense of responsibility that you may have. You can start creating your responsibility pie by writing down how responsible you would feel in the event that something you fear happens. Then, write all possible factors, which may contribute to such fear to happen. Create a circle and mark all pieces of the pie based on the percentage you think should be provided to each factor. Finally, draw and mark the percentage that you are responsible for. Determine if this percentage is relevant to your initial prediction.

The continuum technique can help you construct a better perspective of how you fair for having a "bad" or unpleasant thought. What you can do is to challenge such thought. Say, you have a very bad thought of running over an individual. You can make a list of people who might fit both ends of a continuum. You can label them as the gentlest person and most violent person.

After which, identify yourself in the continuum you made. Determine where you fit on it. Chances are, you may find yourself under the "most violent person." Conversely, as you try to think of people who have done violent acts instead of thoughts, you might re-think and change where you fit in the continuum.

Through the continuum technique, you might realize that you are being too hard on yourself. For instance, you might discover that having violent thoughts is better than acting on them. Eventually, you will be able to acknowledge that it is all right to have a bad thought as long as you do not act on them as compared to other people who commit violent acts.

Finally, the survey method can help you in challenging yourself about the need for certainty. You can do this by carrying out a survey among your family and friends about how well they do on the tasks they have or how they remember things that they read. Whatever you want to survey, compare the results with your initial predictions.

Tool 3: Managing Stress

Given that managing OCD is not an easy task, you may find that your progress would not be as good as expected. In addition, it is highly possible that your OCD can be more compelling whenever you undergo stress. As such, it is best to create a list of stressful situations that can possibly worsen your OCD. You should be able to anticipate what might cause your stress so in the event that it happens, you are prepared. You need to be proactive in reducing your stress through living a healthy lifestyle.

When managing OCD, it is important that you are brave enough to face everything that is associated with it. Once you notice any improvement, make sure to allot time to reward or give yourself credit.

Any progress you make should be followed up by practice. When you keep on practicing the drills and skills of managing OCD, you will soon realize that your obsessive fears have weakened.

Chapter 9: Self-Management of OCD

Aside from availing yourself of assistance from professional mental health therapists, you can also learn how to self-manage your OCD symptoms. Dealing with your symptoms on your own is highly essential because therapists cannot be with you for 24 hours a day every day.

Here are some tips on how to handle your OCD symptoms by yourself:

- ### 1. Learn more about anxiety

The first step is to study about anxiety, what is it, and why and how does a person experience it. It is important to realize that for an OCD sufferer, all of his obsessions and compulsions are driven by this one feeling: anxiety. Since this is the major emotion that you are going to deal with in OCD, you should learn everything about it, including its mechanics, causes, and effects.

- ### 2. Learn more about OCD itself

As you learn more about anxiety, researching on the causes, effects, and other facts about OCD is the next step. This is also important because how can you deal with a problem when you do not know what it is. This book is actually one of the best first literatures that you can read about OCD.

Most of the patients who are suffering from OCD do not have any clue what they are going through so they succumb to harmful approaches in trying to alleviate their obsessions and compulsions.

For example, obsessions are intrusive thoughts that a person interprets in his mind. If you do not know anything about OCD, you may perceive these intrusive thoughts as something else rather than seeing them as they are, just thoughts.

When it comes to compulsions, it would be difficult to plan out effective strategies on how to control your urges if you do not know how you got them or where they come from.

- 3. Look for long-term treatment rather than short-term relief

Majority of OCD patients settle for short-term reliefs to their anxiety problems. This does not help improve the condition, which is why the cycle just goes on over and over again. For instance, a sufferer relieves his fear of germ contamination by washing his hands every time he felt the anxiety behind it.

So, it just continues to become the source of alleviation. Instead of making him control the compulsion, the compulsion controls him even more.

As mentioned in the previous chapter, there are behavioral and cognitive therapies available to treat your condition for the long term. Try and apply them even without the presence of your therapist as well.

- 4. Delay your reactions to your compulsions

One practical way to help improve your condition is to delay your reaction to your compulsions every time you feel them.

Using the same example of an OCD patient with the germ contamination problem, delaying hand-washing for 15 minutes or half an hour could help you gradually eliminate it as your relief ritual. Sooner or later you may do without washing your hands all the time.

- 5. Learn to forgive yourself every time you succumb to your compulsions

No one said that managing OCD is going to be easy.

So, expect to fail a lot of times especially when you are just beginning to deal with your symptoms. Some patients lose hope because they can't seem to get everything right during the first few therapy sessions.

It is okay as long as you continue to do what you have to do. It is much better to take things slowly as the changes will be more long-lasting.

Conclusion

OCPD is a mental health condition that is characterized by a preoccupation with rules, order, organization and control. Those who suffer from OCPD are often unaware that they have a problem as this disorder integrates itself into the patient's personality. These patients display a range of symptoms, including an overly zealous devotion to work, an excessive need for order, a penchant for hoarding, and reluctance to delegate tasks, among others. The symptoms of this disorder cause the patient a great deal of personal stress and places undue strains on the patient's interpersonal relationships.

OCPD includes five subtypes, each with its specific and unique predispositions in personality. These subtypes are knowns as the conscientious compulsive, the bureaucratic compulsive, the parsimonious compulsive, the puritanical compulsive, and the bedeviled compulsive. While each of these subtypes display their disorder in unique ways, all share a compulsive need for order and an extremely high expectation of themselves and others. These unreasonable expectations can negatively impact the patient's life and state of mind, resulting in the need for treatment.

An OCPD patient may choose from different treatment options with the help of a qualified professional. These treatment options include psychotherapy, medication, aromatherapy, cognitive therapy, and more. Many of these treatment methods can be combined to give the patient a greater chance for success in managing their disorder. Patients must come to terms with the fact that they must manage their disorder and that a complete eradication of OCPD is highly unlikely. However, with enough effort, proper treatment, professional help, and support from the family, the OCPD patient can successfully manage the disorder and live a happy and well-adjusted life.

-- Elizabeth Caroline